T0267404

thimbles

thimbles

vanessa shields

Palimpsest Press
1171 Eastlawn Ave.
Windsor, Ontario. N8S 3J1
www.palimpsestpress.ca

Printed and bound in Canada
Book typography by Ellie Hastings
Edited by Abigail Roelens

Palimpsest Press would like to thank the Canada Council for the Arts and the
Ontario Arts Council for their support of our publishing program. We also
acknowledge the assistance of the Government of Ontario through the Ontario
Book Publishing Tax Credit.

A version of *the wine is locked up* is published in Let's Fly Away - A New Collection
of Canadian Poetry, Polar Expressions Publishing, Honourable Mention
A version of *Nonna never complained* is published in *The Bannister*, 2019.
A version of *I want to unfold the disease* is published on *Backstory of the Poem* by
Chris Rice Cooper
(chrisricecooper.blogspot.com/2020/08/vanessa-shieldss-i-want-to-unfold.html)

*And further, there was another prick of the pin: one was wasting one's change; for beauty
spread at one's right hand, at one's left; at one's back too; it was escaping all the time; one
could only offer a thimble to a torrent that could fill baths, lakes.*
Evening Over Sussex: Reflections in a Motor Car, Virginia Woolf

LIBRARY AND ARCHIVES CANADA CATALOGUING IN PUBLICATION

TITLE: Thimbles / Vanessa Shields.
NAMES: Shields, Vanessa, 1978- author.
DESCRIPTION: Poems.
IDENTIFIERS: Canadiana (print) 20210101075
            Canadiana (ebook) 20210101083
ISBN 9781989287767 (SOFTCOVER) | ISBN 9781989287774 (EPUB)
ISBN 9781989287781 (KINDLE) | ISBN 9781989287798 (PDF)

CLASSIFICATION: LCC PS8637.H515 T45 2021 | DDC C811/.6—DC23

Table of Contents

un bacin d'amor

only the good lasts

Dedicated to Maria Giuditta Merlo Bison –
Nonna, Bisnonna, everlasting light.
Thank you for loving me unconditionally.

un bacin d'amor

ponte vecchio

Sign on the old bridge in Bassano Del Grappa, Italy:
"Sul ponte di Bassano noi ci darem la mano ed un bacin d'amor."
On the bridge of Bassano we will hold hands and we'll share a
kiss of love.

memories turn to sound – contralto-heavy moans
carry her back to her Italian mountains
to the old brick mansion with empty squares for windows

in-sucking air
stuccatto
mamamamamama
her inner child emerges lost
in need of a mother turned to dust

pain is an *ohhhhhhhhh*
drawn out like a line with no ending
thickening in the sunrise
waning in the soft afternoons

she points back in time
with her voice
to her bloated house with family food noise wine
to legs that walked waltzed
to hands that held knives fitted to her knuckles
to fingers unbent shining tips thimbled
sewing sewing sewing

inside the moans – disconnected shadows
reconnect to form her Italy
her hips and thighs reach for
broadleaves: chestnut ash birch
mysterious marmots insatiable ibex
larch spruce fir pine prospering in the waiting winters
of her past like swaying ghosts in a death parade

there are still ranges of words clustered like saplings
recognition of faces cracked jokes flirtations
but the moans root in the deeps of her spirit
attempt to choke the seeds of her
past that forget how to take hold

vibrations steady in the *mmmmmm*
lips purse – serious
closing entrances to limestone peaks
in her Dolomite dreams

she is *Ponte Vecchio* Palladio's
architectural gem
blown up and rebuilt again and again

ins and outs of days are rigid in small town northern Italy
caked with mud and hunger
young Maria pleads for an egg at the general store
she walks home with it in her navy wool coat pocket
a delicate secret on her hip

Things die – birds, cats, sisters – and illness
sneaks into Maria's thriving mind
another delicate secret she can feel on her hip

Sickness in the head is worse than poverty
Maria is sent to the house in the mountains
it is as real as the open-air windows
as real as sisters with the same name
as real as fathers who come and go like bee stings
as real as an egg in a navy wool coat pocket

In the mountains Maria's mind is a dress shop
a riveting assembly of delicate designs
patterned secret seeds entrenched in
fresh air frolic and misunderstood freedom

She can go in and out of the house
with the open-air windows
in the mountains
any time she wants

Often she leaves her body
with her sisters while her mind
mends rips in dead soldier's sweaters

Sickness in the head is
a navy wool coat pocket
a germinating seed
a polka-dot dress

a delicate egg

her father came home long enough to make a baby.
Poverty breeds this desperate connection.
Love was a blooming rainbow, intermittent but possible,
enough to keep colours vibrant in the heart, enough to
keep wombs fertile in any kind of body.

Baby Silvana came on a wind – whimpering, wet, wonderful.
Maria, a big sister, not the only one, but the only
one who loved like weather;
constant, fierce, ruby and cobalt.

Silvana grew like radicchio in the garden.
Her laugh the curious wind she arrived on.
Maria protected her but was unprepared
for the flurry of illness, the storm of death.

Silvana returned to the rainbow.

Father came home long enough to make a baby.
Grief breeds this desperate connection.
Love was a cautious cyclamen – ivy-leaved,
hardy and vigorous. Enough to root hope in life,
enough to keep mother breathing, to keep sisters unafraid.

Baby came in a rainstorm – loud and plump like droplets of water.
Maria, a big sister again, not the only one, but the only
one who loved like weather;
steady, determined, seafoam and crimson.

They called her Silvana Two.
She grew like beans in the garden.
Her giggle like the torrential rainstorm she arrived in.
Maria protected her but was unprepared for the slow
giant that would crush Silvana's memories.

Now, the weather is a tree stump and sisters forget
that rainbows can bloom.

her past unravels

I went to school until grade five. I was eleven. My mother told me I had to go with the nuns to learn how to sew. I didn't want to go. I could hear the other kids playing outside as I sewed day and night.

I build a small room in a crumbling rectory attached to a shaken church for Nonna's eleven-year-old self to sew. She sits on a wooden school chair, the remnant of a wrinkled nun's gown resting on her kid-bruised knee; a needle, threaded with skill, pulling up and pushing down practising the perfect baste stitch.

The nuns were twenty-six. They were good to me. Soon we moved to a big room with seventeen other girls in a proper sewing school. The first thing I made were pants for my father. They let us keep the patterns for the clothes we would have to make. I had to make coats. I was a full-time dresser.

The room expands along with Nonna's skills. Her body swivels from child to young woman. For eight years she works in the sewing school.

My father would come home drunk and ask me why I was still going to the sewing school. Why was I still sewing for the nuns?

She is talented. Very talented. And motivated by love. She loves to sew, and she knows it as soon as the voices of the kids playing outside sift and blow away like flour.

I got tips from the nuns. But I was to start working on my own before I was eighteen. Then when I started sewing on my own, the word spread. How good I was. People from the mountains heard of me. People from our small town. Your Nonno...his family was talking about me.

There is the absence of ego as she sews her beginnings. Traces of fear line her story like silk behind wool.

I was making 1-2 outfits a week. It was hard during the war because I had to keep leaving to hide in the mountains. I had to keep stopping. But your Nonno. He lived close to me. I made him a nice blue top. My mother got me a uniform top from a commander in the marines. I turned it inside out and made it like new for Nonno. I sewed for his mother, his sister.

She sews through a world war. Thinks less of the bombs than the bobbins and basting. Thinks about her heart reaching for my Nonno. Handsome. Religious. Soon they will spend time alone together in the mountains.

Nonno stopped me while we were in the mountains. He said, stop right here, and he asked me, do I want to go out with him? He said he'd ask my mother if I could date him.

I can hear in her laugh all the unsaid. She loves him already. She makes him a beautiful shirt between bombings.

While I was sewing in the mountains, he asked my mother if he could date me. When my father found out that we would be together, he was drunk. He called your Nonno the wrong name, but Nonno was too proud to say anything. His pride kept him away from me for three months. I watched him through my window while I sewed at home.

Her cheeks burn with reignited anger and shame. With patience and unconditional love.

Nonno wanted to go to Canada. He'd already done his fifteen months in the military. He didn't have a trade job so he found work in a small ceramic factory making figurines. Then his Zia A sent for him from Canada. It would take three months to prepare the travel. That's when he asked my mother if he could marry me.

We look at a black and white photo of Nonna on a mountain top with her girlfriends. Her smile is bigger than the valley. I can see the mischief in her eyes. A wild young woman with shoulders squared to the horizon – courageous and ready. The fear-twisted threads blow away on the wind.

He left and wrote me two letters a week. They were beautiful and loving. I didn't take them with me because there wasn't room in my trunk. So I burned them. I willingly came to Canada because I loved him and it was the only way to have my life. To marry him.

Before I can stop myself, I ask, did you have any other dreams for your life? She squints.

That's what life was for. To love. To be married. To make a family.

she remembers dates
by tapping her fingers in the air – notes of her past

August 26, 1952 – ocean liner docked in Montreal
September 10, 1952 – train whistled into Windsor

lived with Zia A until the wedding day then
moved into an apartment on Marentette
for 9 months
got pregnant there
in that first month

then a move to Lillian
another upstairs
but this time a kitchen, a bedroom and a shared bathroom
yet another move to share another house
this time with a single rich woman who lived into her 100s
then finally
November 21, 1967 bought this house
the house she still lives in

all the while in the startling in-betweens
between the first birth and the death two months later
between the moves and the pregnancies and the daughters who live
between the cooking and the wine and the self-preservation

she sewed

she transports me to a huge ship
crossing the ocean from Genoa, Italy to Halifax, Canada
ten days on a grand ship tucked in
the underbelly with the third class
   But my friend and I we snuck to first class and got lost in the hallways
her face is twenty again her eyes glassy with mischief
   No, I was never scared   everyone was so nice when we landed in Halifax
   I cried saying goodbye
then three days on the train to Windsor
four weeks later her wedding day
did you know she made her wedding dress
and two bridesmaids dresses?

she turns her face to mine
when the memories float
us back into the present

I love you so much

nonna took me for walks after five-course lunches
after dishes and dancing on fat Sunday afternoons
she took me for walks through the alleys
where the best roses grew reaching through chain link fence
behind the little green-sided house
where the old lady lived – older than Nonna felt like a century

Nonna urged me to *break off what you like*
these ones are for the public on this side of the fence
Nonna's words were gospel and she practiced
reaching into thorny bunches of wine-red roses
keeping the pain of the small stabs in the back of her throat
breaking healthy stems in a fast snap and then lifting
the rose centre to her nose
she is fearless

hand-made apron tied
tightly around her
girdled belly
every day three meals
and feasts for the whole
family on Sundays

crooked-boned feet
in open-toed shoes
swiftly sashaying
across the linoleum
to the beat of some private
mountain wind song
calve muscles pulsing
    bend and lift
    bend and lift
forearms turbulent
waves of muscle
rolling into the
shores of wrists
the pounding of
daily duties
dredging recipes
to life in tired pans
bored pots

a wooden spoon
curved smooth
to the tender
bend between
thumb base
wrapped fingers

this groove a testament to her will
    her service

the day before
her thirtieth birthday
all she could do was cry
certain she would
die at thirty
she had been terrified every
day leading up to it

she cried herself to sleep

the next morning
she awoke
surprised relieved exhausted
alive

Tomorrow is another day
she always said
a haunting mantra
born in the aftermath
of living past thirty

I see Death waiting
patiently in the wrinkles of her skin
I see Love holding a flashlight
shining on another day

after she lets me run up and down the
rainbow-shaped stairs at the orthodox church
she leads me up the street past the empty
field I gallop through in winter snows

an open chain-link fence is an open mouth
into a graveyard – to the left on the path
where fat cherubs and thin headstones
name infants and toddlers and children
their souls barely fluttered before
the pull-back to Mother Sky

Gregory's stone leans to the right
as if being urged under – Gregory
her firstborn named after
Gregory Peck – his baby
breath taken by the crib
unforgivable unblamable
unholdable

she stands in silence heaving her pain
into the crumbling stones
there are no words no tears
just her hand on her thick hip
a moment of remembering a
flicker of anger caught in
the blink of her grey-blue eyes

then a crow hollers and Nonna finds her voice
we sing songs from The Sound of Music
she is my Maria teaching me how to
hold moonbeams in my hands

around the bends and curves
our feet pitter-patter on the
dirt-sky of the Kingdom of the Dead
our laughter keeps the wounded
souls from scaring us away

she wouldn't throw out old stockings
even so darned and re-stitched
they were more scars than skin-tone
but after lunch one Sunday the women
remained at the table among panini crumbs
and chunks of *tighe in tecia*
scattered on the table cloth
we noticed a rip in her stockings

through the telepathy of women
we knew what we had to do

our hands found the rip
our fingers grabbed hold
        And We Pulled

three generations of giggling women
tearing apart what was already broken
opening seams into oceans of bare skin
Nonna's knees knocking as we rocked
shoulders in unison until all that remained
was a golden elastic waistband

tears of laughter tumbled down our cheeks
the men looked at us – confused
I waved a flap
over my head like a prize
a surrender to the bliss of collective undoing

the wrinkle between her eyebrows deepens when she cooks it gathers into the place of the concentration of service of timing of salt of pepper of butter of garlic & spills onto her cheeks & into roses & the crystal wine glass a palm's grasp near she sips down whispers of complaint pausing only to church to sew to bathroom to sleep then back to the service dance   drunk heavy-faced roses sullen pull down from her roots contaminated by everyone else's needs

all those years I watched without knowing absorbing her actions as perfection unaware of what she gave up to give us
I weep for her spirit for the strength it takes
to cook in that kind of kitchen

she made one pantsuit for herself
to wear on a flight from here to somewhere else
or from somewhere else to here
she despised every minute of it
the pantsuit
not the flight

I gave it away as soon as I could

Nonna wore skirts and stockings
no matter the weather or the occasion
a brassiere and a girdle
no matter the outfit or the location
she understood
what to hold
and what to let free

in willistead park she teaches me how to pee at the base
of an elm tree

1. Look around to be sure no one is watching
2. Lift up your skirt
3. Spread your feet into a balanced stance
4. Roll down your stockings to just above your knees, crouch
5. Reach up and pull your girdle to the side
6. Pee
7. Smile

nonna takes a bath in water that barely covers her kneecaps she sits long-legged | her toes like battered arrow tips | the skin on her round belly white like hard-boiled eggs | her belly button a short frown slightly open | darkness inside | among the women her nudity is free | I marvel at the way her red puffy nipples rest on her stomach-top like ripe fruit on a plate | her breasts like white sports socks filled with mangoes | purple-blue veins slide down the sides like juice | I am in the tub with her innocent | curious | she invites me | she wants me there | we wash ourselves | she scrubs my back | I scrub hers | see thick red welts in streams over her shoulders from her bra straps showing me pain she never speaks of | I get cold quickly | even in the scolding water that wrinkles my fingertips into raised roads on maps | she is terrified of water |

she is naked from the waist down. Her skirt & girdle and stockings in a heap on the floor. My undies & pants and socks in a bundle beside the bathtub. She takes the navy washcloth over her open hand, rubs Ivory soap onto it. She crouches a little and washes herself. Tells me to scrub front & back front & back. *Get right in there, clean it good & hard. Then rinse rinse good & hard.* She turns on the tap. Rinses the washcloth. Rinses herself. Rinses the washcloth again. She pulls me toward her. Rubs more Ivory soap onto the washcloth then reaches down & cleans me. It burns. She pulls the cloth away. Rinses it then hands it to me. Rinse she tells me. The hot water on the cloth soothes the burning. *Good* she tells me *very good.*

she said

If God didn't think it was special, he would have put your vagina on your neck.

something happened after her brother died
there was inheritance money
arguments
a trip back to Italy with Nonno
and then his words
we will not go back there
declarative final merciless

her country blocked by
emotions fear commitment
deeper into her cell
she retreated
but quietly
with grace

she never attempted
to leave his prison
didn't know the bars
weren't metal
the locks nonexistent

I didn't ask her
how this made her feel
I didn't think to show
her how to leave

maybe she had it all
figured out
she taught herself
how to leave without
leaving
how to love across oceans
how to mend family
like rips in pant knees

maybe that's why
at the end she knitted
blankets to cover
the gaps

what if this is a lesson in light?
I try nudging Nonna's dignity
forgetting that all this light
comes from the same place

>it comes from her
>she is the light
>she is the sun

I am trees blocking out the sun
rooting in how-could-yous &
you-are-hurting-hers
this ground is a swamp
I am mucking in it

>she is still the light
>she is still the sun

but she can't see
her spirit for its body
she can't see me
rooting away from her
grief is constant heat

is this a lesson in light?
am I a disconnected ray
conceived in a weeping womb?
or has this whole story been
nothing but a tongue of light
describing a refuge?

>if the light comes from her what happens when she dies?
>will I still shine?
>whose tongue will carry her story?

my tongue
my tongue
my tongue

only the good lasts

there are no stories
no one calling attention
to adventures that happened
before we all gather around
the dining room table
no stories about how
Nonna and Nonno arrived
on the shores of a
young ignorant country
no stories about
friendships that traveled
over oceans in
different languages
or army uniforms
shed on dirt floors
like garlic skin

There are no stories
even after tongues
are soaked in
bitter wines and
the freedom to speak
gets smooth
slurs into Italian folk songs

There are no stories
until I ask

when I enter this house
my skin says thank you
my heart settles into the walls
this is the house that saves me

This house has a smell
from a tender recipe of
immigrant Italy
a sanctuary
sustaining me
since childhood

I have come here in sickness
bringing disease & virus
to the lumpy couch to let
the silence protect me
so I could heal

This house isn't perfect
there are flies on the walls
with stories in their hairy legs
impenetrable unswattable
bad things fester in the
dusty curtains

Still this house is my ribcage
the centre that keeps
my centre from cracking but
today I need my eyes to deceive me

I let them work their
powerful denial
I need this house
to remain strong
I need the smell of
peppers swiss chard garlic
pasta & bread to be
my umbilical cord
I need her to
keep feeding me even
as she rots   even as
the smell scars
my nose

When my ribs break
how will I
rebuild through the pain?

her head floats over
the dark brown
faux-fur blanket
she pulls to her chin
soft white skin
in abrupt contrast

her face is a sky
her grey eyes
            darting
constellations

I used to sit in front of
the open window and sew

I lean in
gather her words
like colours
into my ears

I whistled while I sewed
people would stop
look around to see
who was whistling
they thought
I was a man
my whistling
was so good

Then I got these teeth
her hand pushes out from
beneath the brown
blanket brushes her mouth
her face is a storm

and no more whistling

i begin with thimbles

ask her – plastic or metal?
she tells me metal but
plastic works too
we shift to thread
she tells me #56
the best kind for
her sewing machine

it's on the back porch
holding hope for use

I won't find the thimbles
until much later
until I am brave
enough to ask
for them

the wine is locked up
in the cantina in the basement
in damp space where
I used to hide from
fat black crickets
where I fell in the dark
water around
the sump pump

The wine is locked up
in a hand-made wooden box
on a shelf with end-of-the-world
rations   cookies crackers soups
band aids sponges baskets

Cracking rubber boots
rusting bikes
glass jars filled with
dusty longing & her
dead husband's tools
sit in freedom

Nonna wants the wine
she loves wine
why wouldn't she?

Jesus turned water to wine
drank till his heart burst and
resurrected   He never shared
with her but she remained
a fine devoted disciple

Sometimes she sees His
face on the surface
of the dishwater
plunges her
fists into his cheeks
for his lack of sharing

I ask her if she would
drink it all at once
if the wine was unlocked
if she could take it when
she wanted it

she tucked her
gnarled hands
into her elbow bends

Oh no with assurance *oh no*
what's the point of drinking it all at once?

Things last because
she knows how to make them
the marriage the sewing the knitting
all the different kinds of needles

The wine wasn't always
locked up

nonna never complained   not with her heart or her mouth
she took it all like a mountain's cheek takes rain because that's
where she came from   the mountain's cheek   she climbed up
the dolomites two days before she climbed on a ship floated
away from home to the new country   her seamstress fingers
holding needles of hardened memories from a past life   old
thread on a cracked bobbin in ocean winds of change   new
notions measured patterned into a life of abuse   his words
welted her quiet skin   she controlled the pins stitched gowns
she slipped over interior wounds

i found her dressmaker's shears while she was sleeping
i cut into her past & freed up her laughter   i tore into her
present & stopped the dementia   i binded to her future
pried open her spirit so it could rise up to the mountains
in her heaven finally   i knelt beside her rising chest
kissed her soft eyelids & prepared to gather her hidden
complaints   but there were none she smiled then
dreaming of what?   i put her dressmaker's shears
in her bedside table drawer beside the dusty bible & the
stack of darned slippers i took her warm hand in mine
i wept into her   my heart   my mouth   in the woven
fabric of her

i call them episodes
when she freezes
mid-step or sentence
an overlay of
nothingness
pauses her spirit

I can see the disease
like a seam ripper
tearing apart
    connections
in her brain
her eyes
fogging over
vacant
with loss
of patterns

one time
she was walking
from the dining room
toward the chair
in the living room
her legs
moving   then not
her hand gripped
the chair's back
her forehead
lifted into
a sea of skin ripples

I called her name but
her ears were foggy too

for a few seconds
she stood   entranced
in an unanticipated
loss of self

she shook her head
like she had misunderstood
the moments   like she was
rejecting the sudden
mind rip

her spirit snapped
back into her body
like an elastic
she looked at me
deep questions in
her eyes   she was
blinking hard to swat
away the vacancy
her spirit didn't
understand

I rubbed her back gently
felt the hard bones of spine
the thick hump of bent
neck from decades of
sewing   looking down
　　down
creating dresses
pant suits curtains
from patterns
her mind bloomed
like seeds in God's garden

her middle name is Giuditta
she loves to sew
skirts – always skirts
her mind is basting
she loves to knit
blankets scarves slippers for the poor
Malato in testa
her mind tries to mend

I must sew knit
I must fit into her skirts

my hands were always swelling. *I never knew my thimble size. I had 9 or 10 different sizes. Always metal. One day when I was working at home the needle went right through into my middle finger. I had to go to the doctor. I had an infection. So I put the thimble on my ring finger. I had to find my way through.*

I never knew how deeply you loved to sew until I made the time to sit beside you and ask you what you love. Though my child eyes studied your hunched shoulders, your wide back, your elbows poking out on each side, watching the way your fingers never stopped pushing through and pulling out thread. I saw the thimble on your finger but I didn't know

you were our thimble. The metal casing holding us together. The penetrable protection that felt needles go right through your soul. The vessel for infections that no doctor could heal. The love that kept the infections hidden

and now I want to go back retrace discover
understand why I waited until your mind
began to disintegrate before I paid attention
to what you always tried to hide

the thimbles
the infections
the finding
your
way

my hands swell and I see you

this afternoon at 3:45 i jumped in my nonna's head & chased the thought she was trying to grasp see she can't anymore the words melt like hot butter on pasta & all she wants to eat is pasta with butter & garlic & she only eats a full meal at dinner because it comes with wine & the thought of wine is never out of her reach   but this thought the name of my daughter her great granddaughter it was whirling around like a dervish & very difficult for me to catch but i finally captured it in the deep of nonna's temporal lobe   she was giggling skittish   this thought my daughter's name   wrapped in the calm arms of love nonna's best emotion if that's what love is   & then i fell to my knees & wept right there in my nonna's brain   grief holding me like blood holds memories & pain & colours

nonna needs someone to make decisions
or maybe she wants someone to make decisions
I cannot tell and when I look back into
the kitchen the dining room the bathroom
the basement and the church pew
I can't find the line that separates the two

maybe she never wanted to make certain decisions
maybe she was too busy to think about certain things
maybe she was always told it was none of her business
maybe she swallowed the line between need and want
like the gulps of wine before dinner

I don't ask her why she lets things go and go and go
the kitchen the dining room the bathroom
the basement and the church pew   the line is
covered in skin dust disagreements power struggles
that she folds away like Nonno's ironed handkerchiefs

maybe she wanted
to make all the decisions but
it was too hard a fight and so she
made the best decision of all
turn dignity into a pattern
stitch the needs into a shirt sleeve
sew cook clean iron drink and love

these are good decisions

she never changed
the fluffy cotton pad
in the talcum powder
pink plastic case
not for eighty years

she hasn't used the upstairs
bathroom for over a year
the stairs are a devil

now she shuffles to the
commode in the kitchen
her folds loose and inflamed
lonely like the talc

everything changes
around her
I ask if she notices
she doesn't
understand
the question

I go to the upstairs
bathroom   stare at
the pink plastic case
consider how loneliness
attaches to our parts
whether we notice

or not

in the white of the hospital room
Death straddles the window sill
     a waiting storm
I force myself to accept the vibrations
of her knocks on heaven's gate
this is a space for dying and
all I can think to do is tidy her
for the transition

I go to her hands first
palmer and dorsal sides
shades of her soul
in the crooked fingers
that used to create miracles
with thread and faith
     now foreign extremities

I gently clean dried blood
from beneath her hard fingernails
I cut them
file them
massage cream into the dried dermis over
lumpy bones
spongy veins

All this more than
she'd ever gifted herself
these hands never felt a manicure
these nails never felt the colour of red polish
the femininity lurking in the deeps of pampering

In the ghost-silence of the hospital room
we are alone in the healing purgatory of time
I gently wet her hair massage her scalp
hers is a closed-eye ecstasy
in the taming of the itch

i arrive armed with comb scissors
spray bottle leave-in conditioner

A fake story about me as a hairstylist loops in my mind like
the memory of an old perm at the tips of her hair

I believe I'm a hairstylist like I believe she will not die – not today
because today is for cutting her hair

Using extra sheets from the foot of her hospital bed
I wrap her shoulders   spray her hair   soak into her

Playing pretend as I   comb gather cut
comb gather cut   pretend I know what I'm doing

The result is a child's smile on her dusty rose lips
a flirty lash bat as I put my cheek to her face for a photo

later i ask her
if she remembers
what happened
if she can feel

any remnants of the episode
she smiles
I don't
know what you're
talking about

her palm goes to her chin
in an almost flirty gesture
she looks into me
asks for the fifth time
in so many minutes
so the children are in school today?

I nod and smile and lie
because I love her
because I want to
keep her spirit
here

i witness her suffering
displayed like McCall's patterns
in Fabricland windows
gathering like dead skin
in the corners of her
decaying home
her pain
juts like a
misplaced stitch

she is a clothing department
going out of business
colours fading
sizes unfitting
the exaltation
of newness
kind and hopeful
gone

that she said
Love above all
turns my suffering
into an invisible gown
the loss of her
will transform
me to basted stitches

i call to her
she sees the kids
step into the foyer
behind me
she looks at us

her crumb-cornered
mouth explodes
into a smile
I ignore the panic
that rips open
my throat
in the heavy
second it takes
her to remember
my children's names

i am too weak to walk into her house
so I drive by in my dirty car and I look down
her street knowing the distance to her front porch I turn
my head and am welcomed by the sight of her absence

she hasn't been outside since easter when she hurt her leg
another example of me not being there
I feel my dishonour as I drive by and look through the bricks
at her sitting in the chair
her hair too long her nails curled
her mind forgetting to think of me

from my car, I imagine the heat of my love
blowing through the cracks in the double windows
up her nostrils to her brain
and she smells the fragrance of my love
and she tastes the bitterness of my shame
and she smiles

the questions i haven't asked
show up like needles in the rug
reaching for tender sole skin
questions for decades
maybe lifetimes
there is so much I've missed.

I never asked how it felt
the first time you had sex
how it felt to find
your newborn
unbreathing
how it felt to fall
in love with another man
how it felt to watch
your children suffer
how it felt to know
your sister
had dementia
how it felt
to be told
you can never
return to your mountains.

over & over, i am fractured, a crumbling cliffside, a wounded heart – stented – then pinned on your sleeve. Over & over, I swallow my angry words into a pot of boiling wait. Over & over, I tell your eyes to tell your soul to tell your heart that it's okay to let this living go. Over & over, I know that your heart can't hear me. Over & over, I sew my torn needs into an unfinished quilt. Over & over, your thimbles call to me & I am afraid of finding them without you. I am afraid to unpin.

i want to unfold the disease from your eyes
pull away the rotting parts in your brain
I want to tear open the skin on your chest
break open your ribs and memorize your heart

I want to put your liver in my mouth and bite down
taste what you quieted away in your dark organs
I can see your soul quivering on the stairs to your throat
as it chants to your lungs to keep breathing

I decide
to reach
into your body
with my love
carry your soul
to the safety
of my heart
the heart
you taught to be   *extraordinary*
even as it
fails to save you

& there are days my heart has learned how to disconnect from my brain which i am not proud of but the time to be able to breathe without feeling anything is now i can feel *dead* i can feel *gone* this is when i promise myself that i will let you *die* if that's what you need me to do even when no one else can do it someone has to i will do that for you i will give you *death* i will let you *go* & i won't be sorry

the loss of you will be devastating
i will not be able to describe the sadness
it will barely be enough to keep me *alive*
let alone keep you living on in me

i didn't pay attention to her service
until she was no longer able to serve
she was a working woman ahead of her time
lost in the shadowed madness of living in
wartime depravity though there was
no war at least not the kind
with bombs and guns
   with sweeping, bloody deaths smothered in tragedy

full-time work at the hospital with the nuns
then full-time work at home with the family
plus church volunteering and embracing
new immigrants like they were family

she remained steadfast in devotion
to her husband as he lived and died to
her children and to the Good Lord

   What can I get you? she'd repeat
   each empty request a bullet in my chest

i can see your spirit
in the hue of red in your cheek skin
flapping from your shoulder like a loose silk blouse
I can see it out of your body hovering
beside you like an old friend
I wonder if it's always been that shape
wonder how it learned to take his abuse
wonder how it chose to
give so many things up
maybe it's not like that at all
maybe it's more like a protective lining a built-in silk
slippery but efficient
shrinking and expanding with time
I don't know how but I can see your spirit
I thought it needed my permission to go
I gave it in the hospital that day I visited
so sure your body was done its living
so sure your spirit was ready to leap but
I was wrong

It coiled like a stove burner in the kitchen of your soul and waited
I don't know how but I can see your spirit
see it in the waxy undertone of your bent-bone hands
ripping off pieces of itself and stuffing them in my pockets
like dress patterns to be discovered
and made and worn

you are an extension of me

her words dagger into my chest
thrown from a misguided magician's hand
blades breaking through skin
settling into muscle
I know it is not her
           intention
           to inflict
           this agony
loving her now is all pain
today is her ninety-first birthday
how does anyone live that long?
she is showing me
what I dare to receive

as the family gathers
in the dank spaces of
her dilapidating palace
I realize what my job is:

           Benefactor of Extensions
           Court Jester, nay
           Holder of Stories
           Taker of Daggers

eruptions of her legacy
tumble in my blood
her memories
wrap around my ribcage

The good is what lasts

i dream of going into your bedroom
opening the closet door
pulling my fingertips across the
shoulders of your hand-made dresses
I can feel the days it took
you to make these clothes
I can hear what you heard as you sewed
muffled voices on the Price is Right
remnants of Nonno's words shadowing
your daily light like cumulus clouds I

dream I can feel what you felt as you pulled
thread through the bobbin as your
hard-bottomed slipper pressed the motor
for the sewing machine under the table
I can see the shade of soft gold
your soul seeped into each layer
backstitching yourself into every
skirt or dress or shirt from
the tired but generous halls of your
stunning imagination

I was astounded when you told me
you never used store bought patterns
the designs were there behind your eyes
you could draw them into being with
a chalk and a piece of newspaper

I dream of going into your closet
taking your dress blooming with
colourful flowers and memories
of celebrations past and forgetting
I dream of putting on this dress
that it fits me perfectly like you knew
in your deep quiet somewhere somehow
it was meant for my body too

does it make me a bad granddaughter
to refuse this situation?

Does it make me a bad
human to have
taught my heart to deny
certain loves?

Is it okay to hate?

I hate the house
the couch the dust
the diapers the commode
I hate the expired *everything*

When I close my eyes
I see your light
reaching out for me
I see the leaving
of your spirit

I am furious

for two months i did not visit. I did not call. Instead I entombed myself in the catacombs of I can't. Finally, a gifted solution. A plan. That silver shovel returned to my grip. A steady blistering digging out. A pure recognition of need. Needing you. Supple courage. Flexible. Gasping. I walked in the house. Saw you on the chair. Swallowed then fell to my darkness. I squeezed your hand like it was god's. I outpoured. Sobs rolling like exulting waves. And you took it. Took the tears. Took my head. Took my hands. Kissed my forehead. And forgave me.

who will take her things?
the gold ring with the round ruby stone
the gold chain with the etched saint on a gold pendant

the sewing machine
the cracked plastic yogurt
container filled with mismatched buttons
the slippers bras nightgowns
everything she made for herself

what is really *hers*?
how does a thing belong to a soul?

when her body leaves
how long will her life
remain in the things
she used?

I will take her
flowered dress
her bike

I will take her
thimbles

i stole your flowered dress and your striped blue skirt.
but I asked you for your thimble.
Of course, see if you can find it on the back porch.

Winter cold caressed my face as I felt for the light,
then illumination and operatic angels in my ears.
There it waited like an open stone on a holy cave – your sewing machine.
Down on bended knees, I brought my body to look for your thimble.

I gasped –
not one, but two.
Two thimbles.

if thimbles could speak
what would they say?
I know there is salt in your thimble
bitter wine-crusted yearning
for the days when
all it wanted was to be filled by you

on my left arm there's a thimble in black
ink needled into my skin
the side of my body that
holds my heart protected
by lungs & ribs & blood & muscle

protected by a brain that works
to remember who you were
before I let you down
I live inside the thimble   hiding
in the metal round as your body
forgets to love itself I become so
afraid of you dying my sight is coloured
by the silvers of our sanctuary crumbling
my tongue dries on the dust of the words
that held our family together

kitchen pasta sugo polenta
dishes dancing wine scrabble
books wheel of fortune church
love & love & love

in the purgatory of a transitioning soul – confusion
the soul's identity becomes
a dried sheet on the clothesline of life
stiffening stifled by 4pm on a dry hot day in June
the soul is thirsty impatient
curiosity escalates into fear
wonders why the wind still whips
when the weight of water is long gone

i stare at nonna
as I lean against the back
of the lazy boy

she's in bed
her limbs like yarn
her cheeks pink skies in morning

I stare because it's all I can do
witness this
tragedy of a body
emaciated
around a soul
banging against the
fleshy walls
of its shrinking prison

she opens her eyes
her lids are velvet curtains

Hey, look at your sexy standing
she says
smiles

Nonna. My extraordinary Nonna.

one day i'm going to walk into her house and she won't
know me

who is this person? she'll ask
fear behind her eyes

I'll walk to her slowly
smile

I'm someone who loves you I'll tell her
I'm someone who loves you

minds change like colour in heated cotton
time fades all courage unless
I lift us
hang our colours on the line
trust we will survive the weather

what if all she ever wanted was a quiet lifting?
to feel her children run through the sheets
laughing
loving

pinching wooden clothespins across generations

on this day she is different – again
I cannot arrive prepared
for the versions of Nonna

on this day my instinct is
to hold her hard-boned hand to
gently press my palm over
her heart chakra
to whisper
it's okay

she ignites in anger
Basta! she growls
I pull away
You want me to stop touching you?
she nods yes
I do not know this version

seconds later – recognition
I love you
I blink fear out of my eyes
pray she will not notice
my panic my desperation
I love you

don't force her to get up
keep her in bed
order the special air mattress
that will stop the sore from spreading
cut out the backs of her nightgowns
add another blanket to the pile

she is always cold

food is a nuisance
try applesauce
she chokes
offer ice cream
she denies the sweet
sensation

she begs for water
cold water

the palliative care doctor is a man

That man is handsome, who is he?
A half-whisper.
I'm by her side in the dining room while the others
gather in the living room. The television is on.
Muted.
He's your new doctor.
She closes her eyes, but not her ears.
I wait. I watch.
What are they talking about?
Food.
Why are they here?
For you.
She shakes her head. Two more times she asks me
the doctor's name.
It'll take me three months to remember his name.
I burst out a laugh.
What are they talking about now?
Medicine.
Why?
For you.

I'm fine. No fussing.

The doctor comes to Nonna's bedside.
She smiles up at him. He asks
Can I take your blood pressure?

I have two arms. She holds them up.

The doctor presses and palms.
How do you feel, Maria?

Empty.

Later, she rustles her arm under the blanket.
I gently take it out and rest it on her chest.
She knocks on my belly with her knuckles.

It's your fault, this belly. These boobs too. You gave them to me.
She shakes her head.
I'm sorry
Through a smile.
I grab her hand and put it on my heart.
No! I love it all because it's from you!

Her response
so perfect so profound
I cannot hold it.
Her love is a vibration
burying into my sternum

a constant hum.

three daughters one granddaughter a nurse
in the dusty dining room tomb
Nonna's stiff naked body on its side
for a washing

one daughter holds Nonna's thin-skinned shoulders
caresses her face
that contorts in discomfort
chiselled *why?* lines on her forehead
wide eyes searching for heaven her mother
a voiceless open mouth

one daughter holds Nonna's hip
sharp enough to be a weapon
duty-driven hands
eyes darting between the past
and the future
the now excruciates

one daughter makes a sandwich
in the kitchen then leans in
the doorway biting hard
chewing violently

I hold the juxtapositions on my tongue
taste the languages of their different loves

there's a hole at the base of Nonna's spine
an open wound where her spirit slips out in thick goodbyes
the nurse pulls a cloth over it

Nonna's muscles tense in rejection
her body says what I know but
will not speak

I swallow her silent fight

i curse my inability to speak my heart
to point and dagger at all the wrongs
I pull out my hair and heave
it in faces so full of fear they stone

my courage is blue-inked in half-cursive
filling gold-edged pages in fancy-covered journals
safe in the silence of a narrative no one reads but me

I pray for her to die so the lying will stop
so I can let the holes between my ribs
canyon

her pain is spiritual
boiling in the sauces of her cells
like *sugo con carne* on the stove of her life

palliative:
relieving pain without dealing with the cause of the condition

the cause of the condition is separation
spirit from vessel
time from breath
mother from child

the cause of the condition began at birth
climbed up mountains
motored over oceans
gathered in steady
recipes of leavings

this lifetime of loss
sewn then knitted
into wine-soaked sadness
masquerading as devotion
fickle faith she turned to song
was there ever any relief?

end of life:
medical care options, primarily for patients who are considered
critically ill

her soul is critically ill but
what of the patient suffering lifetimes of patience?
she does not want to go because we don't want her to
it is not up to her
it never has been

I wait for her body to take its final stand and
metamorphose into a perfect sewing needle
that dazzles on the dirty carpet top
a lesson

nonna's spirit floats above

what is left of her body
connecting at her left earlobe
her right thumb knuckle
her upper lip
her lower intestine
the centre of each of her Achilles tendons

she is threads of light
strings of frayed emotions
argument spit   dangling
to live longer
to die now

I can hear her fear flexing
solar plexus pleas
please don't take me yet

her cheeks metal
dimples like the tip of a thimble

even though

starvation ploughs
what remains of her
she takes my breath away
     I give it to her

even as
I weep through the
devastating sadness
of her
confrontation with
The End
       she persists in her remaining

even though
her endings are shape-shifters
re-ignitions of story
lace-locked legacies
mending old pains
into new – this truth is that

even her
final stitch on
the hem of my soul
is precise –
violently awakened
proof of her determined love

water gets inserted into Nonna's
open mouth with a syringe
Nonna is a frail bird
with a tongue so swollen with need
she does not talk
only yells
mama!

the windows to her soul are petrified-stained glass
I am a moving shadow to be feared

the medical term is "agitation"
it's bullshit
the correct term is "fight"

Nonna does not want to die
this fact is true
precise

her purpose is to love
and she cannot love if she is dead
she fights against her body on the
desert battlefield of time
her soul is trapped in a
rotting vessel and all she can
do is beg for water that will
not sustain and plead for her
dead mother who is a
dazzling mirage

I don't believe she sees heaven
I don't believe she sees
"the light"

she *is* light
Nonna does not want to die

i undo myself

cut out emotions like
patterns for gowns and
I peel off layers of what I
cannot be
so I can breathe
pretend that I am okay
fake that I have the strength
for this unbearable perishing
I stitch the fragments
of our steady undoings
into an apron of agony
while Nonna's spirit
reaches back and
unzips from her body

I will take over as lead seamstress

this is a plea: in your next life please find me

Follow the threads
I have planted in the
mountains of your
oldest memories –
they are the strongest
they will survive
beyond this life

Follow the thimbles
I have dropped like seeds
in the wounds of your soul –
there will be a garden in the
landscape of your
next life

I have used the same threads
the same thimbles –
planted
so I can survive beyond
this life too

This is a plea: in your next life please find me

We will tend to each other
cultivate differently –
better

her body becomes

a realm
slowly
separating
from the motherland

her propensity
for living is
beyond our
control now
we sink into
the quaking
of severing

the End is of the body

her cheekbones are
hardcovers on an ancient book
her eyes all curtains and broken windows
her lips serpent skin peeling

to awake is a startling sorrow
hours are marathons of moaning
sleep is a border crossing
her body is an ocean liner
death at the helm

i can measure her proximity to It
by her mouth
always open now
a slight slit sundered

her mouth is an open door
hinges rotted off –
an inviting entrance
for the It that wants
to take her

send in the opioids to calm the garrison
the fighting withdrawal is in effect
her battlefield body defeated

her spirit pulls the shroud
white Italian silk

a truce

i let her go before she goes

does a soul need permission to leave?
to wither & let go its grasp on this
version of life's branch?

to feel a severing from the ones
that love it? need it? think
they can't exist without it?

I can't exist without her
but she can't exist like this –
an overflowing thimble
beautifully escaping our grasp

i am afraid of my cell phone
it is a line to Death
perched on my dashboard
while I drive

I pretend that she is already dead
to see how my body will react
the pain is extraordinary

I imagine myself smashing
into the cement divider
air sucking out of the car
I fly and I am free

My cell phone rings

domani è un altro giorno

my cell phone rings at 6:12am
thursday, June 25th

I answer
> *knowing*

the sounds that release from my body
scare my daughter

the language of loss is wordless

i give you permission to never be the same I give you permission to never fill the space that resides in your centre like an unfilled freshly dug casket hole I give you permission to curse death to continue to exist to continue to breathe

without Her.

her forehead is still warm
cheeks a sighing pink
her stillness   impossible

I kiss her

it takes too long for the nurse to arrive
Nonna's body grays
cools to death's coldness
        grief hot as hell's flames

there is talk of tying it
with a *canevasa*
to pull the jaw up
[close the door]
just a body now

the absurdity of it all

black body bag gaping on a stretcher
the first graveyard
two young attendants
begin the taking

I hide in the kitchen
     terrified shaking nauseated

white cotton sheet shroud
breathable durable soft
I look once
see her feet socked in purple fleece

hear the zipper –
its chain of teeth
     its closing mouth
     a final hymn

thursdays will always be cracked
slivered open into the beyond
into the space where angels weave
new wings for souls fresh out of broken bodies

thursdays will always pinch that tender
flesh behind my elbow
>   *it is real*
>   *you are no longer here*
>   *in your self*

deep in the pain of remembering
I climb up the mountains of grief
the terrain of our memories jagged
slippery
tricky
exhausted
my upper body strength – depleted

my heart is an ocean of
infinite thursdays

today
is a question mark infused to my spine
    I hunch into it

the pandemic funeral is a pain-storm of eyes

noses
mouths
chins shrouded

     fear and loss
     like family
     gathered & grieving

i take three pictures of you in the casket
but it is not you in the casket
the face misshapen the
hands bright orange

I am asked to send the pictures
to family in Italy

I don't – it's not you
it's not fair

Months later
the pictures line up like prisoners as I scroll

seven hours of visitation
every hour on the hour
evacuate for disinfecting

people drone in like vibrating memories
by appointment only

everyone breaks the rules
hands grip in sadness
arms embrace heaving shoulders
masks touch in covered-mouth kisses

Nonna stands courageous on her favourite mountain in Italy
our mourning a songbird's trill caressing her earlobe

someone tucked roses from the bouquet on your casket
into the bunch of fake yellow gerberas on the side of your tombstone

brittle stems and paper-dry petals wither toward your smiling face
in the black and white photo of you and Nonno

the roses ache for your light

the date of your death is not yet carved
on your side of the gravestone
your birthdate: september 15, 1928
bold & beautiful
but your death date: june 25, 2020

    a ghost

will you remember the date you
shifted?

I keep thinking it was the 26th
the round belly of the six taking
hold in my memory
for a reason I can't comprehend

you remembered dates like
invisible notes in the songs
of your life
tapping the air with your
fingers to conjure your past

I think I can't remember the date
because I can't let you go

a shirtless man with 1980s hair
walks over to me
as I sit in front of your tombstone
Who are you here for?
he asks politely
My Nonna
I point at her photo

Bison, he reads, pronounces *Bees-On*
he looks for her death date
She just passed
Oh, they haven't engraved the date yet?
No
I remember when they were digging, he says

cue my imploding heart

Bowing a little, *my deepest sympathies*
Thank you
and I bury bury bury
my pain –

     I feel you smiling
     for summoning a shirtless man to your grave

the ground is bumpy
more weeds than grass cover the hole
that holds her fancy casket
there's a pair of crickets at the base
of the large black stone
serenading my sadness in
an insect symphony of despair
on the edge of a Wednesday morning

where are you, Nonna?
I don't feel you here
amidst the dusty dead
the ground is ground
knowing your corpse is
six feet under me
is absurd
unfair

why bury what is so bright?
maybe you are the sun

the simple truth is
that I miss you so much
everything about you
that words can and can't express
      your body
      your grace
the list is unworthy
impossible

i want you back in the kitchen

dressed in the black skirt & flowered shirt you made yourself
belly taut & covered by another hand-made garment
the apron – your superhero cape

I want you back in the kitchen
cooking a ridiculous meal
loads of food for a load of family
timed perfectly to topple into bowls
to feast while everything is still hot
the mashed potatoes
the *tige in tecia*
our hunger
our weakness

I want you back in the kitchen
puckering and patting your lips
after a gulp of *vino* – a long *ahhhhhhh*
a raised eyebrow
a wink & a smile
for me

breakfast with nonna in the graveyard
yellow jackets curiously hover
groundskeepers dishonour the quiet
with tractors and trucks
their words dirty the peace-needing air

life protrudes into every place
the living are loud

it is my responsibility to tell her story
she didn't ask me to
and that is why
I will

because love lives beyond one body
into another and another and another

It is my responsibility to extend
the story of the perfect disease
incurable in its glory
to resurrect the pain from
the deeps where the
language of your essence
moves like blood

ask me anything, children
take my hand from stirring the *sugo*
lead me out of the kitchen onto the front porch
pull me down beside you to sit and
ask me anything

You see me every day and
there is a book for this story we are in
there are books for stories before you
a book for the story that made you a
book for the story that brought me your father a book
for the stories of my childhood –
so different from your own

Ask me anything, children
any time any where
because a body is made of books
this is how we stand up
      on the words of our past

Ask me anything, children
I want you to know me
like you know how to breathe so
you understand the difference
between an inhale and an exhale
a gasp a shortness a *holding in*

A letting go

response: when i die i want your thimble on my finger

When I die I want your thimble on my finger
pushed on tightly so it feels my heartbeat
so my heartbeat can match the memory of your heartbeat
that pulsed through the thimble and created dresses that changed lives

Response: When I Die I Want Your Thimble On My Finger

The love you give spreads over me like silk
the voice of your wisdom sings onto my lips
the song of memories you stitch into my soul
the melodies unite us like bumping clouds in heaven

Response: When I Die I Want Your Thimble On My Finger

What you love I keep on loving in your loving honour
I carry your light in my lashes so when I cry I can weep
your love back into Being – storms of you rush out of me
sometimes I gather tears in your thimble

Response: When I Die I Want Your Thimble On My Finger

I love you the hardest the deepest the most
because that's how you love me – and it is pure
when I die I want your thimble on my finger
so I can find you and we can begin to sew again

Closure: The area of the garment that opens and closes for dressing. Also called opening.

Pg. 298, The Complete Photo Guide to Sewing by Nancy Langdon. 3rd Edition

Acknowledgements

In the fall of 2018, I was overjoyed to find out that the Palimpsest Press family would publish a very different, but still rooted-in-love version of this poetry collection. Aimee, thank you for believing in me, in my story, in my words. Abby, dear editor, thank you for your patience and understanding. Thank you for your precision and compassion. It's been a long journey...one in which we both lost people we love...I believe this brought us together more deeply.

A writer's family is large. It has to be. The words need to be gathered into different souls, the poetry needs to be loved by different hearts. Thank you to the incredible Humber Summer Workshop family who were the first to open their minds and hearts to my Nonna's legacy: Cathrin, Nick, Aimie, Taneet, Sue, Susan, Marie-Claire, Erinn and Kyo. Especially Kyo, for your gentle wisdom. Especially Erinn – soul-sister, life coach, dirty-fingernail pal.

Thank you to my Write Sisters, Penny-Anne and Karen, who help me navigate the long hallways of enlightenment.

Thank you, Christopher, BF, soulmate...for everything.

Thank you, Charis. Sister, this collection has your sparkles all over it. (Oh, the thimbolism!) Thank you for always retreating with me – inside and out.

Thank you, Jane. Your wisdom continues to shape my writing life and soul.

Rebecca, my Queen, I love you. That's all.

Lin, we are family.

Thank you, Kerrie, my heart is fuller because of you.

Thank you writers from Gertrude's Writing Room who helped shape many of the poems in this collection. Thank you for letting me cry all over the place. Peter, Irene, Margaret, Dee, Kerry, Deb, Candice, Mary, Nolan, Ruth-Ann. Sweet Alley, thank you for being a constant beacon of intelligence, passion and love.

Alice...just...oof and eep and soooo much love.

Mom, the light in me honours the light in you. Thank you for borning me.

Jett and Miller, as always, this is for you. Ask me anything, always. Nick, my true love, thank you for loving me.

Thank you Ontario Arts Council and the recommending publishers who read an early rendition of this collection. Acknowledging writers financially and in good faith changes everything.

Indeed, it will be close to three years by the time this book is in our hands. We needed the time to learn, to share, to grieve, to love.

Nonna, I love you. Thank you for your unconditional love.

Vanessa Shields is the owner of Gertrude's Writing Room — A Gathering Place for Writers. You can find her mentoring, editing, teaching and writing at Gertrude's or having a dance party in her kitchen with her handsome husband, two amazing kids, and two golden retrievers. Visit her website: www.vanessashields.com.